# Beekeeping

# The Essential Beekeeping Guide: A Step-By-Step Guide to Beekeeping for Beginners and Advanced

## Andy Jacobson

# Contents

# Foreword

Are you ready for a captivating bee-venture? Beekeeping is an empowering hobby and the rewards are plentiful. Besides contributing to saving the honey bee from extinction through healthy beehive practices, you also receive some of nature's sweetest gifts: delicious honey and nourishing beeswax. On top of this, keeping bees will ensure your garden is always well-pollinated and therefore more fruitful. Beekeepers will no doubt witness a significant increase in the productivity of their garden – from faster growing rates to an increase in the quantity and size of fruit, vegetables, and flowers. You'll be stunned by the huge difference these pollinators make!

I am thrilled to introduce you to the ancient hobby that is beekeeping. The art of beekeeping is an extremely rewarding practice and contrary to common belief, extremely safe and easy. All you need is some guidance to get you started and this is exactly what this guide provides.

In this essential guide, we will cover an introduction to beekeeping, all you need to know about your bees, how to set up your first bee colony, how to safely manage and inspect your beehive, how to raise your bees, seasonal beekeeping tasks, how to harvest honey and beeswax, how to make beeswax body lotion and candles, and much more!

Not only will you be introduced to the essentials of beekeeping, but I will also share with you the challenges I had in my first years of beekeeping, and how to overcome them. This guide is equipped with photos and diagrams to facilitate your understanding. For new beekeepers, I recommend reading this book in the order it has been structured with. This will put you on a steady path to learning and mastering the wondrous art of beekeeping!

Best wishes,

Andy Jacobson

# Section 1: Beekeeping – An Introduction

There are number of sweet reasons to keep honeybees. Not only are bees silent and odorless, they also require almost no space. This makes beekeeping a hobby which you can pursue regardless of whether you live rurally or in a city. Furthermore, if you have your own garden, having bees will make sure that your garden is always well pollinated and fruitful.

Besides boosting yields in your garden, there are also many health benefits associated to honey bee products. Both honey and propolis have antibacterial qualities. Royal jelly is extremely rich in B vitamins and pollen, high in protein, also provides a remedy for seasonal pollen allergies.

On top of this, the practice of beekeeping is both stress-relieving and calming. And once your bees are fully settled, they will do most of the work for you! While inspections are necessary to maintain a healthy and productive hive, inspecting your beehive and observing your bees is a magical and exciting spectacle.

Although the honey bee's greatest contribution to our environment is by way of pollination, the most sought-after crop for backyard beekeepers is honey.

Honey is a much healthier sugar substitute. Just like wine or coffee however, honey is without flavor in itself. It is the nectar from different flowers which creates different honey flavors. If you want to produce mono-floral honey, that is honey that is from just one type of flower, you must place your hive in an area where that flower dominates. Bees who are hived amid an orange grove for example, make orange-blossom honey, while bees in a field of clover will make clover honey. As soon as the flower blossoms, harvest your honey.

While mono-floral honey is beautiful and delicious, wildflower honey is equally if not more wonderful, unique and special at the same time. Wildflower honey is made from a natural blend of different flowers. The color and flavor of your honey will vary from harvest to harvest and that's one of the beauty's of beekeeping. In *Section 8* of this guide, you'll find step-by-step instructions on how to go about harvesting this liquid gold.

On top of this you get beeswax which you can use to make candles and skin care products. Beeswax candles have a delightfully sweet aroma while beeswax moisturizer protects and softens your skin. Some of my favorite beeswax recipes are found in *Section 7.*

A common concern among new beekeepers is the apprehension of being stung. If you were stung before, it was probably by a hornet or a yellow jacket, which are aggressive and volatile insects. Honey bees in contrast, are gentle and non-aggressive creatures. The chances of being stung by a honey bee are therefore extremely slim. Honey bees only ever use their stingers as a last resort in order to defend their colony – and the die immediately after stinging. When they are away from their hive and defending the beehive is not a priority, they therefore docile and friendly.

On top of this, if you are diligent and watchful of the inspection tips and techniques covered in *Section 5* of this guide, you can ensure never to be subjected to stings. Sloppiness on the other hand, can increase the likeliness of stings. But as humans, we naturally built a tolerance against bee stings – the more stings you get, the lesser the impact of itching and swelling.

There are many different types of honey bees. Which honey bee is best suited to your needs and preferences is something we will cover in the next section.

# Section 2: Bee Basics

Once your hive is set up, your bees will do most of the work. Your role as a beekeeper are therefore limited. Nevertheless, it's important to know what's going on in your hive. On top of this, it's also very interesting!

Over the summer, there will be approximately 60,000+ bees in a healthy hive. There are three castes of bees: the queen bee, female worker bees, and male drone bees. Each bee caste has their own characteristics, roles, and responsibilities.

## 1. <u>Three Castes of Bees</u>

### The Queen Bee

There is usually one one queen per colony and everything that goes on in the hive centers around the queen bee. The queen bee is the only reproductive female in the bee colony. Her main task is therefore to lay eggs for the hive. Every spring, the queen bee will go on mating flights during which she mates with male bees from the hive. She then stays in the hive laying eggs, sometimes as many as 1500 a day! However, not every egg she lays will be fertilized. Fertilized eggs become worker bees while unfertilized eggs become drone bees.

The queen bee is the largest bee in the hive and has a lifespan of around five years. Queen bees are usually only productive for around two years and egg production decreases the older she gets. Because of this, many hive owners will replace their queen bee every fall in order to keep up a vibrant and productive hive (see *Section 5* on hive maintenance). Left to their own however, the hive will naturally rear a new queen once the older bee queen stops being productive.

## Worker Bees

Workers bees are highly non-reproductive female bees. Worker bees born in the spring or summer only have a lifespan of around 6 weeks. In the first three weeks of their life, they are referred to as 'house bees'. House bees are responsible for all the in-hive tasks, such as cleaning the hive, feeding the queen, and storing the nectar and pollen from foraging bees in the hive, among other things. After three weeks, worker bees become 'field bees' and start foraging for pollen, nectar, propolis, and water.
Worker bees which reach maturity in the fall can live up to 4 months. Their role over the winter is to cluster around the queen bee and keep her warm. Come spring, they help her raise the first batch of newborn bees.

## Drone Bees

Male bees are referred to as drones. A drone bee is almost twice the size of a worker bee. Drones have large eyes that cover almost their whole head and don't have a stinger.

Their sole task its to mate with the queen bee. Drone bees die after the mating process and any drones left in the hive in the winter are made to leave the hive by the worker bees so that they don't consume precious hive resources during the winter months.

## 2. <u>Choosing the Right Honey Bee For You</u>

There are many different kinds – races and hybrids – of honey bees. Below is a list of the most common honey bee kinds which are readily available to purchase, along with their characteristics which will help you in your decision.

- **The Italian bee:** These bees are yellow-brown with very distinct dark bands. Italian honey bees are the favored bee kind as they are excellent honey and comb producers and are also less prone to disease. On the downside however, they are known to consume surplus honey if not removed immediately after the honey flow has stopped and are known to rob weaker neighboring colonies of their honey supplies which can spread diseases among hives. Italian bees maintain a large winter colony which requires large stores of food.

  **Summary:**
  - o Gentleness: Average
  - o Honey processing: Very good
  - o Propolis: Low

- Disease tolerance:       Average
- Spring build-up:        Good
- Overwintering ability:   Good
- Other traits:           Heavy honey
  robbing

- **The Caucasian bee:** Caucasian bees are dark colored with gray bands who frequently rob the honey stores of neighboring hives. They are native to the foothills of the Ural Mountains in eastern Europe and are able to withstand harsh winters. If you decide to opt for Caucasian bees, make sure to medicate them with Fumigilin-B every spring and autumn as they can fall victim to Nosema disease.

**Summary:**

- Gentleness:          High
- Honey processing:     Low

o Propolis:                  High
o Disease tolerance:      Average
o Spring build-up:         Very low
o Overwintering ability:   Average

- **The Carniolan bee:** Carniolan bees are also among the most widely honey bees used today. These are dark-colored that hail from the mountains of Austria and Yugoslavia which tend to rapidly increase in population size. These are very docile bees and can be worked with with little smoke and protective clothing. They don't tend to rob other colonies of honey and maintain a small winter colony, which therefore requires only small stores of food. They are extremely good at building beeswax, but do have do have a tendency to swarm which may leave the beekeeper with a poor honey crop.

**Summary:**
- o Gentleness: High
- o Honey processing: Good
- o Propolis: Low
- o Disease tolerance: Average
- o Spring build-up: Very Good
- o Overwintering ability: Good

- **The Russian bee:** These bees are said to have fewer than half the mites compared to other bee races. A study lead by USDA researches seemed to show a resistance to both varreo and tracheal mites. Russian bees also tend to decrease brood production when nectar and pollen is in short supply. This results in a smaller winter colony which makes them better at surviving the winter and colder climates.

**Summary:**
- o Gentleness: Average
- o Honey processing: Average
- o Propolis: Average
- o Disease tolerance: Good
- o Spring build-up: Average
- o Overwintering ability: Very Good

- **<u>The Buckfast bee:</u>** The Buckfast bee is a hybrid bee from southwestern England which is now easily available in the US. They produce good honey crops and are very good at housekeeping which reduces their proneness to disease. On the downside however, they are moderately defensive and only exhibit a comparatively slow spring population buildup.

**Summary:**
- Gentleness:          Low - Average
- Honey processing:    Good
- Propolis:           Low
- Disease tolerance:    Good
- Spring build-up:     Low
- Overwintering ability:  Good

There are also many other hybrid bees available commercially. When opting for hybrid bees however, make sure to re-queen regularly. Allowing natural queen replacement to occur can lead to a defensive and difficult to manage colony.

When choosing which strain of bee to go for, do keep in mind that there is not one 'best' kind of bee. Which honey bee is right for you will depend on the traits you favored by yourself. If you're after very gentle bees, your choice is between the Carniolan and the Caucasian bee. If your goal is honey production, go for the Italian bee. If disease-resistance and hardiness to harsh winters is your priority, your choice is between the Russian and the Buckfast bee.

Now that we have a sound understanding of the traits of different strains of honey bees, this is now a great time to start exploring everything you need to know about your beehive, and cover all the beekeeping tools you need to get started!

# Section 3: Beehive Essentials and Beekeeping Tools

Before building your own beehive, make sure to check with your local zoning board and make sure you're authorized to keep bees in your neighborhood. While most communities open-minded and will welcome new bee colonies, some communities may have imposed zoning and legal restrictions on beekeeping.

**Initial investment:**

- A package of bees and a queen will cost around $60 to $80 (see *Section 4*).
- You can either build your own hive or you can purchase one commercially for around $200 to $400. Commercially purchased hives will usually come with all the equipment, tools and medication you'll need.

## 1. **Your beehive**

While building your own beehive can be an exciting and often more cost-effective venture, I only recommend doing so if you're extremely good at carpentry. Beehives require exact measurements and it is therefore recommended, and also more time-efficient, to just purchase a pre-fabricated one.

The traditional beehive is called the Langstroth hive. While there are other beehive designs, such as the top-bar hive and the warre beehive, Langstroth hives are standardized and it's therefore much easier to find a solution in the face of specific problems. On top of this, honey extractors are build to exclusively work with Langstroth frames, which makes honey harvesting significantly easier. The honey harvest you receive with a Langstroth hive is also significantly greater compared to the other beehive designs.

You may wish to experiment with other hive designs once you have honed your beekeeping skills and you may even want to build your own beehive. However, for the learning beekeeper, the Langstroth hive is the 'go-to' design.

## The Langstroth hive

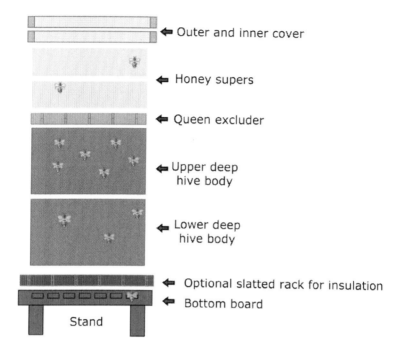

Outer and inner cover

Honey supers

Queen excluder

Upper deep hive body

Lower deep hive body

Optional slatted rack for insulation

Bottom board

Stand

This is the essential structure of the Langstroth beehive. Do note however that when beginning your beekeeping journey, you will start with only one deep hive body. The second one will be added once your bee colony has reached sufficient population growth to support a second hive body, which is usually after 6-8 weeks. We will discuss when and how to add the second deep hive body in *Section 6* of this guide.

Now that you have an understanding of the structure of your beehive, it's time to talk about all the tools and accessories you need to kick-start your beekeeping adventure!

## 2. Essential beekeeping tools:

### Smoker

You'll need your smoker every time you visit the hive and it will allow you to inspect your hive safely. The smoker is a fire chamber which produces a lot of cool smoke which calms your bees. It is recommended to get a smoker made of stainless steel and to only use a little smoke at a time.

## Hive Tool

You will also need your hive tool every time you visit your hive. You will need your hive tool to open your hive, loosen hive parts and manipulate frame. You will also use it to scrape off the wax and propolis from the woodenware.

## Bee-Proof Clothing

Make sure to wear long pants, high boots and a long-sleeved shirt when investing your hive. Remember to choose light clothing as bees don't like dark colors.

## Veil

Always wear a veil when visiting your beehive. Although honey bees are gentle and rarely sting, they do love exploring – especially dark holes such as nostrils and ear canals.

## Gloves

You can either use gardening gloves or purchase long-sleeved beekeeping gloves. When installing your bees or during hive inspections however, it is actually advised not to use gloves. Gloves are in fact counterproductive and make you clumsier.

The only times when you need to use gloves are:

- During the honey gravest when your bees are more protective over their honey.
- When moving hives.

- Near the end of the season when your colony is at its strongest.

During inspections when there is a propolis, it is recommended to use disposable latex gloves. These are readily available at pharmacies, don't affect your agility and keep your hands clean with working with sticky propolis.

## Alcohol

When going on inspections, keep a plastic spray bottle with rubbing alcohol on you. Use this to clean any sticky honey or pollen of your hands.

## Baby Powder

Dust your hands with baby powder before going on inspections. Honey bees like the smell of baby powder.

# 3. <u>Optional beekeeping accessories</u>

## A Hive Stand

Although this is not a necessity, having your hive on an elevated hive stand means no bending over during inspections. This makes the hive a lot easier to work with. It also protects your bees from a dampness and from ground-based pests.

Elevated hive stands are something you can easily build yourself. Alternatively, you can place your beehive on cinder blocks.

## A Slatted Rack

You may wish to insert a slatted rack between the bottom board of your beehive and the lower deep-hive body. This will allow for excellent air circulation and also prevents cold air from reaching the front of your beehive.

## A Screened Bottom Board

This board replaces the standard bottom board. It improves ventilation in your beehive thereby keeping your bees calm. The screened bottom board also come with a sticky board. Mites attached to the bees naturally fall of the bees each day and fall to the bottom of the beehive. These mites would normally crawl back up and re-attach themselves on the bees. With a screen bottom board however, they would either fall to the ground or get stuck on the sticky board. Screened bottom boards therefore reduce any potential varroa mite problems that might otherwise plague the beehive.

## A Frame Rest

A frame rest is a very useful device which hangs down the side of your beehive. It provides a secure and convenient place on which you can rest frames during inspections.

## A Bee Brush

This brush allows you to remove bees from frames and from your clothing without harming them.

**A Toolbox**

To keep all your tools neat and ready-to-go for when you embark on your beehive inspections.

# 4. <u>Where to Position Your Beehive</u>

In theory, you can keep your hive pretty much anywhere. Below however is a list of criteria will contribute to the most optimal environment for your bees. While you might not be able to fulfill all of these, even a few will make a positive difference on the well-being of your hive.

- ☐ Face your hive towards the southeast – this means your bees will rise early and have longer to go foraging.
- ☐ Provide shelter and protection form the wind at the rear of your hive – erecting a windbreak will reduce the stress that heavy winds can cause to your colony.
- ☐ Place your hive on firm and dry land. Make sure your hive is same-levelled from side to side with the front of your hive slightly lower than the back. This will ensure that rainwater drains out of the hive.
- ☐ Allow for good ventilation in your hive, for example, by using a screened bottom board instead of a standard bottom board.

☐ Place your hive somewhere where it will receive both sunlight and shade – try and avoid both very sunny and very shady spots.

☐ Make sure there is a nearby water source for your bees to access. If you don't live near a stream or pond, make sure to provide a water source for your bees.

# Section 4: Obtaining and Setting Up Your First Bee Colony

The process of obtaining your bees and putting them into their new beehive is called 'hiving'. Hiving your bees is in fact a very easy process. In this section, we will talk about how to purchase your bees, how to feed your bees, how to make honey bee syrup, and what to do when it comes to hiving your bees!

## 1. **Obtaining Your Bees**

### Ordering a package of bees

The best option available to beekeepers starting a new beehive is to order a package of bees. When ordering a package of bees, your bees will arrive in a box (approximately the size of a shoebox) equipped with a syrup water dispenser and a separate cage for the queen. Make sure to purchase your bee package from a reputable dealer and when ordering your package, make sure to order a marked queen. If you order a marked queen that means she'll have a colored dot painted on her thorax. The dot will help you spot the queen during inspections. By discovering an unmarked queen, you'll also know that the queen you installed has gone and that a new bee queen has taken her place.

If you're ordering a package of bees, try to order them as soon as possible. Packaged bees are in limited supply and ordering as early as the November/December for a spring delivery will avoid any potential disappointment.

## Purchasing a nuc

Another option is to buy a **nucleus (nuc)** colony of bees from a local beekeeper. A nuc is a small wooden box which contains three to five frames with broods, bees and a productive queen. When you receive your nuc, all you do is transfer the frames into your own beehive. While installing bees this way is significantly easier and also less stressful for the bees, finding a beekeeper who has nucs for sale can be difficult.

On top of the above options, you can also buy established colonies from a local beekeeper. If you're new to beekeeping however, it is recommended not to purchase an already established colony. Not only do you miss out on all the little aspects of building a new bee colony, but already established colonies are also more protective over their hive and you are therefore more likely to get stung. If you do choose to buy an already established colony however, it is absolutely necessary to make sure the colony you're purchasing is disease-free.

## 2. <u>Taking Your Bees Home</u>

If you've ordered a package of bees, the below are steps to follow.

Before your bees arrive:

☐ Your supplier will tell you approximately when they will ship your package of bees.

☐ Package of bees are rarely shipped straight to your home.

☐ The week before the estimated date of arrival, make sure to inform you local post office that you are having bees shipped and provide them with your telephone numbers.

☐ Instruct the people at the post office to keep your package of bees in a cool and dark place until you arrive.

The day your bees arrive:

1. Inspect your package for any dead bees. Some dead bees are to be expected, but if you find more of an inch of dead bees at the bottom of your package, make sure to fill out a form at your local post office and to call your vendor and report the findings. He should replace your bees.

2. Take the bees home straight away and when you get home, spray your package of bees with cool water using a spray bottle.

3. Leave the package of bees in a cool place for an hour. Your bees will be both hot, thirsty and tired from their journey.

4. After the hour, spray your package of bees with sugar syrup (non-medicated).

## 3. <u>Feeding Your Bees</u>

You only need to feed your bees twice a year – once in the spring and once in the autumn. Provided you have purchased your bees from a reputable beekeeper, they should already be medicated for the first season. In your second season however, you may wish to feed your bees medicated syrup twice a year (once in the spring and once in the autumn).

Below are easy-to-follow bee sugar syrup recipes which you can easily prepare in your own kitchen:

**Non-Medicated Syrup:**

1. Bring 2 and a half quarts of water on your kitchen stove to a rolling boil.
2. Once it comes to boil, turn the heat off and add 5 pounds of white granulated sugar to the water. Make sure the stove is off so to avoid the sugar from caramelizing which can make your bees sick.
3. Stir the sugar water until all the sugar has completely dissolved.
4. Let the syrup cool to room temperature before feeding it to your bees.

**Medicated Syrup:**

1. Mix 1 teaspoon of Fumigilin-B in approximately half a cup of cool water.
2. Prepare non-medicated syrup following the instructions above.
3. Leave the syrup cool to temperature.
4. Add the medicated water to the syrup and stir.
5. For added health benefits, you can also add two tablespoons of Honey B healthy to your bee food.

For feeding your bees once they are settled in their beehive, it is recommended to use a hive-top feeder.

# 4. **Installing a New Colony into the Hive**

It's best to hive your bees in the late afternoon on the same day on which you received your bees. Make sure it's a clear day. If it's windy, rainy or cold, it's best to wait a day or two. While they're waiting to be hived however, make sure to spray them 2-3 times a da with sugar syrup.

Below are 20 steps to follow when hiving your bees. Make sure to read over these steps again and again and to follow the steps in that exact order:

1. 30 minutes before hiving your bees, spray them with generously non-medicated sugar syrup without overdoing it.

2. Make sure to wear your veil as well as 'bee-proof clothing' (please refer back to *Section 3*).
3. Using your hive tool, lift the cover off the package. Pull all staples or nails out of the wood cover.
4. Jar the package down on its bottom. Your bees will fall to the bottom of the package.
5. Remove the sugar water dispenser and the queen cage and loosely place the cover back on the package.

6. Examine the queen to see whether she is ok. If your queen has died, you should be able to order replacement queen from your supplier at no extra cost.
7. Slowly slide the metal disc on the queen cage to the side.
   o Remove the cork at the end of the cage to see whether there is a white candy in the hole.

- o If the white candy is present, remove the entire disc.
- o If the candy is not present, you can use a small piece of marshmallow to fill the hole.
- o If your bee package comes with a strip of Apistan, then remove this from the back of your queen cage.

8. There will be two small frame nails bent at a right angle. Bend these into the shape of a hanging bracket.

9. Spray your bees again and jar the package down a second time. this again will cause your bees to fall to the bottom. Bees become loud during installing which is completely normal. Spray them again with sugar water if you need – you will see that by spraying them with syrup, they will be very calm.

10. Prepare your beehive. Remove five frames and keep these nearby (ideally on hive stand).

11. Hang the queen cage with the candy side up (it's very important that the candy side is up!) between the center-most frame and the next frame. Make sure that the screen side of the queen cage is facing the center of the hive.

12. Spray your bees once more with syrup water.

13. Jar the package down, take the cover of the package and jiggle and pour around half your bees straight above the hanging queen cage.

14. Jiggle and pour the other half of your bees into the open area created by the five missing frames which you have put aside in Step 10.

15. Once your bees have started spreading across the area, slowly put the frames back into the beehive. Make sure to do so carefully so you don't crush any of your bees.
16. Place the inner cover on the beehive.
17. Place the hive-top feeder on top of the beehive
18. Close off the inner cover's half-moon ventilation space with a clump of grass. Remove only once your bees have become established in their new home.
19. Place the outer cover on top of your beehive.
20. Lastly, insert your entrance reducer but leave a 2cm opening for your bees.

You're finally done! It's time to take a breath and relax. Leave your bees undisturbed for a week, don't peek as this disturbance may lead to your bees killing their queen, and observe your hive only from a distance.

This is also where all the fun begins! You can start seeing your colony building itself, you'll notice foraging bees flying in and out of the hive, you'll see guard bees protecting the entrance of the hive, among many other wonders!

Before we move on to how to inspect your beehive and successfully manage your honey bee colony, here is some essential guidance on how to use the entrance reducer:

- ☐ For about four weeks after hiving your bees, leave the opening at around 2cm (see step 20) to allow your bees to build up their numbers at which stage they will be able to defend a larger hive opening.
- ☐ Leave the entrance reducer in place for around six weeks after which you can position it so that the largest opening is utilized.
- ☐ You can remove the entrance reducer completely after around eight weeks. At this point, your bee colony should be strong enough to defend a fully opened hive entrance.
- ☐ You can put the entrance reducer back in during cold weather (use the largest opening) to prevent heat from escaping the beehive.
- ☐ In warm temperatures of 60 °F and above, make sure to remove the entrance reducer.

Andy Jacobson

# Section 5: Safely Inspecting and Managing Your Hive

Congratulations, your bee colony is installed and you are now crowned a true beekeeper! Once your bees are installed, they will be doing most of the work. Taking your first peek into the hive is an incredibly exciting experience. Your first hive inspection is the moment at which you can start building a relationship with your bees. Because of this, it's a good idea to develop good habits early. In this section, I will cover all essential inspection techniques you need to safely inspect your hive. Stay calm, relax, and enjoy this incredibly amazing spectacle!

If you are new to beekeeping, try and visit your bees once a week so you get a hang of the process as well as a chance to observe the life cycles of your bees. For the more experienced beekeeper, 6 to 8 inspections a year is more than sufficient. It's best not to disturb your bees too often as this sets honey production back slightly with every inspection.

## 1. Hive-Inspection Tips:

Here are some simple hive-inspecting tips to follow and stick with:

**Before going to inspect your hive:**

- ☐ Wear light-colored clothing only. Bees don't like dark colors.
- ☐ When visiting your hive, always wear a veil.
- ☐ Make sure to avoid strong odors on yourself and your clothing. Take a shower, brush your teeth and don't use perfumes, colognes, or any other strong scents. Remove any jewelry and anything made of leather or wool. Bees don't like any material made from other animals.
- ☐ When visiting your hive, always use your smoker. Light your smoker before going on your inspection and make sure the smoke that comes out of your smoker is cool. Just like the spraying syrup, the smoker will keep your bees calm and friendly.
- ☐ Bring your toolbox (see *Section 3*) and an old towel to every inspection.

## When inspecting your hive:

- ☐ Inspect your hive only during the day and only when the weather is pleasant.
- ☐ Never leave honey or syrup in an open container near your hive.
- ☐ Take your time – bees don't like sudden movements.
- ☐ Allow the bees to crawl on your clothing and don't swat at them.

## 2. <u>Opening Your Hive</u>

Always approach your hive with calm and assured steps from the side or rear of the hive. Avoid approaching the hive from the front as you don't want to run into inward and outward flying bees.

1. Standing on the side of your hive, approximately 2-3 feet away from it, blow a few puffs of cool smoke into the entrance of the hive to calm the guard bees. Be generous but don't overdo it.
2. Still standing on the side of your hive, lift the hive cover up and blow some cold smoke into the hive. This is to calm any guard bees at the top of the hive.
3. Place the smoker on the ground and slowly remove the outer cover with both hands. Make sure to get a good grip and place the cover upside down on the ground next to you.

If you're still feeding your bees at the time of inspection, you will also need to remove the hive-top feeder. To remove the hive-top feeder, follow the following steps:

1. Blow some cool smoke through the screened access into the hive.
2. Use your hive tool to separate the feeder from the hive body. These two parts may stick together, but regardless of this, make sure to ease the parts apart gently so as to avoid alerting your bees.

3. If you're having trouble removing the feeder, loosen both sides with your hive tool and blow some cool smoke into the crack that form as you loosen it with your hive tool.
4. Wait 20-40 seconds and remove the feeder and place on the ground.
5. When removing the feeder, make sure not to spill any of the syrup. If syrup remains in the feeder, cover the feeder with the old towel you brought with you.

Number one rule of thumb of beekeeping is to *never* leave syrup out in the open. This can attract neighboring colonies and can cause war (quite literally). If you're no longer using a hive-top feeder, you'll need to remove the inner cover which is always used in the absence of a hive-top feeder.

☐ To remove the inner cover, blow some smoke into your hive through the oval hole.
☐ Using your give tool, gently release the inner cover from the beehive. Again, if you're having trouble removing the inner cover, loosen both sides using the hive tool. Pry the inner cover from the beehive body slowly and quietly.
☐ Blow some cool smoke into the cracks that form as you loosen the inner cover from the hive body.
☐ Wait 20-40 seconds and remove the inner cover. Lean it against your hive but be careful not to crush any of your bees.

Now that your inner cover (or hive-top feeder) is removed, your hive is finally open! It's now time to take a peek into the magical life of your bees.

Upon opening the hive, slowly blow several puffs of smoke down into the hive. Make sure the smoke descends down into the spaces between the frames. Most of your bees should at this point move toward the bottom of the hive.

You don't want to keep the hive open for longer than around 10 to 15 minutes. What you will have to do during inspection will be discussed in the next section.

## 3. <u>**What to Do During Inspections**</u>

Inspecting your hive is essentially the same every time you visit your hive. Always start by removing the first frame from whichever side. To remove the wall frame (your first frame), follow the steps below:

1. Use your hive tool to loosen the wall frame on both sides.
2. Using both hands, slowly pick the first frame by both ends and carefully life it out.
3. If you have a frame rest, store your wall frame there. Alternatively, lean it vertically up against the body of the beehive.

Now that you have removed the wall frame, this gives you the space to manipulate the other frames. Slowly work through the frames of your hive. Use the same procedure to loosen the second frame and once inspected, return it to the space where the wall frame was located. Repeat this for the third frame and after inspection, place it into the open slot where your second frame was originally located. During this process, make sure not to crush any of your bees and push them aside with your fingers or the flat end of your hive tool if necessary. A small blow of smoke will also make them move out of the way.

Make sure to get a good grip on your frames – the last thing you want to do is drop a frame that is covered with your bees. Inspect both sides of your frame and make sure that all movement you make are slow and controlled. Especially when turning the frame to inspect the other side, make sure to do so slowly.

Also if you notice your bees have all lined up in a row between the frames, this is a sign that they could do with another blow of smoke to disperse them.

## 4. **What to Look for During Inspections**

Inspecting your frames correctly is crucial to the art of beekeeping. The purpose of inspections is to determine the health of your colony. In this section, we will cover what to look out for at every hive visit.

**Checking for your bee queen:**

> Every time you visit your hive, always check for whether your queen is alive and productive. If you manage to find your queen that's great, but remember that a single beehive will house around 60.000 bees in the peak of summer. Locating your queen can there be hard and time-consuming. So rather than looking for your queen, it's better to look for eggs. Eggs are translucent white in color and somewhat resemble a grain of rice (see left side of the picture below).

To make spotting the eggs easier, you can use a normal magnifying glass or binocular magnifiers. Binocular magnifiers can be worn under your veil and tipped to the side whenever you're not using them.

**Inspect your honeycomb cells:**

Every time you visit your hive, make sure to take a note of what is going on in the cells of the comb. Each frame of comb will contain about 3500 cells on each side. Inspecting these cells will give you a good indication of the health of your bees. Look out for larvae, capped brood, pollen and nectar. These are all indications that your hive is in good health and productive.

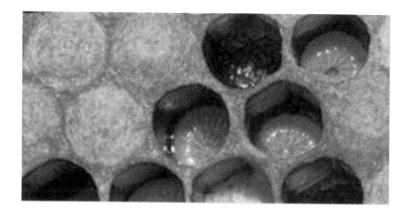

In the above image, you can see the bee babies on the right – these are called larvae which are singularly curled into a cell.

To the left you can see capped brood. Capped brood are larvae cells which have been capped with a wax cover. The wax cover is porous, allowing the bee babies to spin cocoons and develop into pupae.

**Recognize the food collected by your bees:**

Another thing to look out for are nectar and pollen. To master the art of beekeeping, it's important to learn and recognize the various food stores of your honey bees.

Pollen comes in great variety of colors: orange, brown, gray, yellow, blue, etc. In the image below, to the right of the capped brood, you can see pollen of various colors stored in the honeycomb cells. Cells that look 'wet' may contain nectar or honey. During hot summer months, bees will store water to keep the hive cool. Some cells will also contain honey. These cells will look white and airtight.

## Examining Brood Pattern:

Another important aspect to inspect are brood patterns. A compact and tight brood pattern will mean that your queen is in good health. Spotty brood patterns on the other hand, is a sign that your queen is ill or that you have an old queen which needs replacing.

A loose brood pattern like in the image below is an indication that your queen needs replacing. Sunken or hollow brood cells are potentially a sign of brood disease in which case you'll have to medicate your bees.

## 5. <u>Closing Your Hive</u>

Once you're done inspecting your frames, you'll have to return the first frame back into the hive. In order to put the first frame back into the hive, follow the steps here:

1. Blow some smoke onto your bees to calm them down.
2. Push all your other frames toward the opposite wall of the beehive. This will make sure that all frames are at the exact same position they were in before the inspection.

3. Pick up the firm frame that is either hanging on your hive stand or leaning against the hive. If you can still see bees on this frame, make sure to gently move them away guiding them towards the hive entrance.

4. Slowly slide the first frame back into the hive. Use your hive tool to adjust the spaces between the frames.

If you're using a hive-top feeder, place it back on the hive body. Top up with sugar syrup if it's running low and replace the outer cover. If you're not using a hive-top feeder, you will have to go through steps 5 and 6 first before reaching the seventh and final step.

5. Remove all the bees from the inner cover which should be lying on the ground next to you.

6. Replace the inner cover on the hive by sliding it in from the rear of the beehive. Make sure not to crush any bees.

7. Replace the outer cover. Again, make sure the outer cover is free of bees before sliding it back from the rear of the hive toward the front of the hive, along the inner cover. Push any bees out of the way and make sure the ventilation notch on the outer cover is not blocked.

And you are done! Inspecting your beehive for the first time can be daunting. I would suggest either writing these steps down, taking the book with you, or having someone read out the steps from a distance (if they're not wearing a veil).

After your first few inspections, all these steps will become more fluid and you'll start gaining a better insight into the lives of your bees. A final piece of advice is to just have fun and most importantly, stay calm and relaxed. Nothing disastrous can happen. If your bees get a little excited, just blow an extra few puffs of cool smoke at them!

The above are guidelines to 'routine inspections'. On top of these routine tasks however, there are additional things to look out for in the first eight weeks after hiving your new colony, as well as seasonal tasks, which will be covered in the next section.

# Section 6: New Colony Check-Up and Seasonal Tasks

In this section we will talk about the other start-up tasks and check-ups that are necessary during the first eight weeks after installing your new colony. We will then move on to seasonal check-ups and tasks. Do remember however that these tasks are to be performed *on top of the routine inspection techniques* discussed in the *Section 5.*

## 1. The First Eight Weeks of Your Colony

There are a couple of special beekeeping tasks which need to be performed in the weeks following a newly installed colony. As mentioned earlier, you should leave your hive undisturbed for one week following hiving.

**Week 1:**

Once the week has passed however, it's time for your first inspection. On top of performing the inspecting tasks outlined in *Section 5*, there are a couple of things you need to do and look out for:

- **Make sure the queen was released from her cage.** Look into the hole where the candy plug was originally located. If the candy is gone, this is a great sign that some of your worker bees have opened and released the queen from the cage. Take the cage and place it near the entrance of the hive.

- **Remove any burr comb that you find in the gap created by the queen cage.**
  Although this burr comb is lovely-looking (see picture below), it is very important that you remove this as failing to do so will create problems in the future.

When removing the comb, make sure your queen is not on it. If she is on the comb, you must slowly place it back into the hive. Gently move her off the burr comb. Once your queen is removed from the burr comb, you will also have to remove all the other bees by gently shaking it. You can take the burr comb back with you.

- **Look for eggs.**
  If eggs are already present, this is a good indication that your bee queen is already productive. If you find eggs, then that is perfect. Close the hive and leave your bees to work for another week or two until your next inspection. If you're new to beekeeping, I would highly recommend taking magnifier with you. Eggs are very very small and hard to find, especially when you're new to beekeeping.

**Week 2-3:**

- **Look for larvae.**
  Your eggs should now have developed into larvae, one each curled into a honeycomb cell.

- **See how well your queen is doing.**
  If after 2-3 weeks you see two single-sided frames filled with bee babies, she's performing averagely. Less than that is an indication that your queen may need replacing. During the third week, you should also see capped brood which means your bee babies

are at the final stage of their development.

- **Top up your feeder with syrup if necessary.**

- **Look for queen cells.**
  Bees create queen cells (also called supersedure cells) if they think their queen isn't productive enough and this is an indication that the bees are planning on replacing their queen. If you find more than 3 to 5 queen cells, it's time to order a new queen. From experience, giving the bees a new queen is better than allowing them to create a new queen.

- **Look for swarm cells.**
  Bees create swarm cells to prepare for swarming. This is usually a sign that the hive is too overcrowded. If you spot one swarm cell, don't be too concerned. But if you find eight or more swarm cells. This is a fairly accurate indication that your colony is planning to swarm. If you spot an increasing amount of swarm cells, add your second deep hive body as soon as possible. How to add a second deep hive body will be discussed shortly. Also try to improve ventilation.

Queen cells and swarm cells look very similar. Queen cells however are located in the upper two-thirds of the frame while swarm cells are located along the bottom third of the frame.

## Week 4 - 8:

For new beekeepers, I would recommend visiting your hive once a week. This gives you a chance to get to know your bee's life cycle and to really understanding the workings of the hive. At every inspection, follow the routine inspection tasks as outlined in the previous section.

After 4 weeks however, provided everything has been running smoothly so far, and **7 out of 10 frames** have been modeled into comb, it is necessary to add your second deep hive body.

To add your second deep hive body, follow the steps below:

1. Blow cool smoke into your hive as you would during a routine inspection.
2. Remove the outer cover and the inner cover (or hive-top feeder if you're using this instead of the inner cover).
3. Place the second deep hive body on top of the first hive body and fill with ten frames and foundation.
4. Slide the hive-top feeder on top of the new deep hive body and top up with sugary syrup if necessary.
5. Slide the outer cover back in place from the rear of the hive on too of the hive-top feeder.

In your 6th to 8th week, you want to keep looking out for queen cells and for swarm cells. On top of this, you'll also want to try and improve ventilation. The below are a couple of extra tasks to be performed in week 6-8:

- **Open up the hive entrance to allow for better ventilation.**
  You can do this repositioning the entrance reducer to allow for an opening of about 10 cm. In the eight week, you can remove the entrance reducer completely. Your colony is now strong enough to defend itself.

- **Manipulate the frames to encourage your bees to draw more comb cells**.
  To do so you can move any unworked frames between frames of newly drawn comb. However, try not to place these right in the middle of your hive as you don't want to disrupt the environment of your brood cells.

- **Add a shallow honey super with frames and foundation to your hive**.
  At the beginning of your eight week, once seven of your frames are worked, you can remove the hive-top feeder and add a shallow honey super and a queen excluder to your hive.

## 2. **Seasonal 'To-Do's'**

As seasons change, so do the duties of a beekeeper. This is part of the natural process of beekeeping and it keep it exciting year in year out.

## In the Summer:

☐ Visit your hive every two weeks in the summer. This is to make sure it's healthy and that your queen is well and working hard.
☐ Add honey supers as required.
☐ Keep up with swarm control during the hot summer months! This is when your bee population is at its peak.
☐ Look out for honey robberies.
☐ Harvest your honey at the end of the nectar flow (we will discuss how to harvest your honey in *Section 8* of this guide).

## In the Autumn:

☐ Analyze the honey stock and determine whether your bees have enough honey. Ensure the upper deep hive is filled with honey to ensure that your bees will withstand the winter. If your winters are short, make sure to keep 30-40 pounds of honey in the hive. If you have harsher winters, try and reserve about 60 pounds or more of honey.
☐ Feed and medicate your bees using the recipe in *Section 4.*

☐ Provide ventilation using various ventilation techniques, e.g. by adding a ventilation box on top of your hive. A ventilation box is essentially a wooden box filled with burlap stapled to the bottom which contains wood shavings, straw and other material which absorbs moisture. Place it above the inner cover or above the brood box to prevent the chances of dampness building up.

☐ If you have harsh winters, wrap your beehive in black tar paper which will absorb heat from the sun and help your colony control temperatures inside the hive. Use two layers of tar paper on the top of the hive and place a rock on it to avoid it from blowing off. Keep the entrance and the upper ventilation holes uncovered.

☐ Erect a windbreak if possible and add a mouse guard to the entrance of your hive.

**In the Winter:**

☐ Make sure your bees have enough food. Don't open the hive - just take a peek inside. If you don't see any honey in the top frames, it's time for some emergency feeding. Once you start feeding them, keep feeding them until they start collecting their own food in the form of nectar and pollen.

☐ Keep an eye on the hive entrance. Remove any snow and dead bees that may be blocking the entrance

☐ Order a package of bees if necessary.

☐ The quiet winter time is also a great time of the year to be undertaking other bee-related DIY projects, such as making your own body lotion and candles– step-by-step instructions on how to make these will be covered in *Section 9.*

**In the Spring:**

- See whether your bees have made it through the winter. Fingers crossed! When inspecting make sure to do so quickly so as not to allow too much cool air to enter the hive.
- Make sure your bee queen is still alive and well. Can you see any brood or eggs? If so, that's a good sign.
- Make sure your bees still have sufficient food.
- A few weeks before flowering starts, medicate and feed the bee colony. the first two gallons of feed should be medicated with Fumigilin B (follow the recipe in *Section 3*). All subsequent feed should be non-medicated.
- Look out for any swarm cells.
- Rotate your hive bodies.

During the course of the winter, the bees will slowly move up and cluster near the top of the hive, where the honey is located. The bottom hive at this stage will be empty of both honey and bees. As colonies expand, they will become congested and move upwards if there's a second hive body. They are however not likely to move down. Because of this, it is important to rotate your hive bodies. To do so, follow the steps below:

1. Wait until night temperatures are milder before rotating your hive bodies.
2. Wait for a mild and sunny day (at least 50 degrees Fahrenheit) and open your hive using the smoker as you would during a routine inspection.
3. Place the outer cover on the ground next to you and remove the upper deep hive body.
4. Remove the lower deep hive body (which should now be empty) and clean the bottom board.
5. Add a slated rack on top of your clean bottom board. This is not absolutely necessary but will help with hive insulation for the upcoming season.
6. Now place the deep hive body with all your bees on slated rack (if you added one) or the clean bottom board.
7. Blow some puffs of smoke on your bees and replace the inner and outer covers.

In about 2-3 weeks, it is recommended to restore the original hive configuration, placing the deep hive bodes back into their original positions. At this point, provided our bees have already been bringing food to the hive and you have stopped feeding them, you can also add one or two honey supers to your hive.

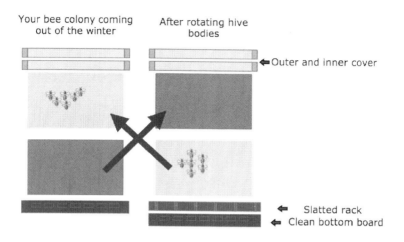

# Section 7: Troubleshooting

In this section, we will talk about what to do in the face of the most common beekeeping conundrums. The parts covered in this section are problems commonly encountered. The best way of dealing with them is through anticipation - anticipate, and act quickly!

## 1. <u>Swarming</u>

Swarming is when roughly half your colony gets up and disappears with the queen. Obviously, this is something you would want to avoid. Because of this, it is important to anticipate swarming and to look for swarm cells as an early indication that your bees are thinking about swarming (see previous section).

There are two main reasons that may cause your bees to swarm – congestion and poor ventilation. In order to avoid swarming therefore, there are a couple of things you can do:

☐ **Avoid congestion:**
To avoid congestion, it is advised to add a queen excluder as well as honey supers in early spring - before the nectar flows. Before adding the honey supers, stop feeding and medicating your bees. Another thing you can do to avoid congestion is by

rotating the deep hive bodies in early spring (as explained in the previous section).

☐ **Provide good ventilation:**
There are many different ways in which you can improve ventilation in your hive, such as making sure the ventilation hole in the inner cover is open. To further improve ventilation, you can also drill small holes in your honey suppers and in the upper deep hive body and thereby improve air ventilation.

☐ **Replace your queen every autumn:**
Bee colonies with younger queens are generally less likely to swarm.

☐ **Make bees comfortable in hot weather:**
You can do this by supplying a nearby water source. Also make sure the hive isn't located in the full sun. For the best place to locate your beehive, refer back to *Section 3* of this guide.

☐ **Remove queen swarm cells:**
Make sure to remove all queen swarm cells and do so using the sharp end of your hive tool. Your bees won't swarm without a new queen in place.

## 2. <u>Absconding</u>

Absconding is when all your bees leave the hive. This is a very unfortunate situation and sadly, there is not much you can do other than order a new package of bees and wait for the new seasons to start. However, it's important to be aware of the most common causes of absconding, and thereby anticipate and prevent:

- **Colony Collapse Disorder (CCD):**
  This is a very recent phenomenon and the causes of which are as of today unknown. Many causes are currently being considered, including fungi and pesticides. Nevertheless, the best way to avoid CCD is simply by making sure your colonies are strong and by causing as little stress as possible to your bees. This includes providing adequate ventilation, feeding your bees when there is a limited supply of nectar and pollen, and upholding good beekeeping practices.

- **Loss of the Queen:**
  It is therefore important to check for eggs and other signs of your queen's presence every time you inspect your hive.

- **Lack of food:**
  Always make sure to provide your bees with honey syrup feed whenever the supply of nectar and pollen is scarce.

- **Uncomfortable Living conditions:**
  Make sure your beehive is located in an ideal location.

Do refer back to *Section 3* on where to locate your beehive.

- **Pests, mites and disease:**
  Routinely medicate your bees to prevent any problems associated to pests, mites and disease. Be wary however only to medicate your bees before the honey supers are placed on the hive and after they are removed from the hive.

## 3. <u>**Losing Your Queen**</u>

As soon as you notice that your queen is gone, you have two options. You can either let nature take it's course and have your colony create their own queen, or you can order one in, which is the faster option. There are certain benefits to ordering in a new queen. Not only is it considerably faster, but you can also be sure that your new queen is fertile and that she has desirable characteristics. Leaving your bees to replace their own queen can lead to less desirable characteristics.

To introduce the new queen to your beehive, remove one middle frame from your deep hive body and hang the queen cage in the empty space, just like you did when hiving your new colony (see *Section 4*). Leave your bees be for one week and then inspect. Once the week has passed, inspect your hive to see whether the queen has been released and has been laying eggs.

## 4. <u>Honey robberies</u>

Robberies occur when one beehive is attacked by another colony. Robbing is something you certainly want to avoid, not only does it ruin the chemistry inside your hive, but it also often ends in many bee casualties. If your colony is unable to defend itself, it also means that all your sweet honey will be gone!

**Spotting a robbery:**

Robbing bees are relatively easy to spot. They will approach the hive empty-handed and leave the hive weighed down with nectar. Foraging bees on the other hand, enter the hive with nectar or pollen and leave the hive empty-handed. When a robbery is taking place, you'll also see fighting at the entrance of your hive.

## Preventing and stopping a robbery:

If the robbery is already happening, there are a couple of things you can do to put an end on the attach. Reduce the size of the entrance so that only a single bee at a time can enter and exit the hive. This will give your colony a better chance at defending itself. If the temperature is hot, make sure to provide extra ventilation. Another thing you can do is to soak a bed sheet in water and cover the hive when it's under attack. Remove the sheet after a day or two, at which point the robbery should have ceased.

In order to prevent robbery in the first place, make sure to never leave an open container with honey out somewhere near the hive. This stimulates robbing behavior. It's also important to keep the hive entrance restricted until your colony has grown strong enough to defend itself.

Unless you're really unlucky, you shouldn't need to deal with the above problems provided you keep up good beekeeping practices. Lastly, before moving on to the fun bit of beekeeping – harvesting honey and beeswax – it's important to note that bees, like humans, get sick. It is therefore important to look out for any signs that may give an indication as to the health of your hive every time you inspect your hive. To avoid sickness, it is recommended to medicate your bees yearly. Remember however that you should never medicate your bees while there is honey in the hive which will be consumed by humans. Therefore, medicate only before honey supers go on the hive and after they are removed (see *Section 6*).

# Section 8: Harvesting Honey and Beeswax

It's time for the honey! At this stage you've done all the work to maintain your colony's health and kept your bees honey. Now it's time for some sweet rewards! What is more, home-grown honey is also significantly more delicious and healthier than commercial honey. In this section, we will cover how to go about harvesting and extracting your honey.

If you're in your first year of beekeeping and it's the first season for your new colony, just beware that your honey harvest will be relatively small. This is because new colonies need a full season to build up enough population that will allow them to gather surplus honey.

Before moving on. It is worth noting that there are two main types of honey which you can harvest: extracted honey and comb honey.

- **Extracted honey** is the most common type of honey. Extracted honey is honey which is removed from the honeycomb using centrifugal force (through using an extractor). It is then bottled in liquid form.

- **Comb honey** entails harvesting the honey with the comb. Comb honey – that is both the wax and the honey – is entirely edible.

For new beekeepers however, I would stick with harvesting extracted honey. This is because in order to harvest comb honey, absolute perfect conditions are required – that is, you must have a strong hive population which is extremely productive and you must also have ideal weather and very good nectar supply.

Because of this, we will start by talking about how to harvest extracted honey.

## 1. **Timing**

The most common time to harvest honey is when the hive is filled with capped and cured honey. I would recommend looking into your honey supers every now and then to see how your little bees are progressing. If roughly 80% or more of your honey suppers are filled with sealed (that is capped) honey, then it's time to start harvesting!

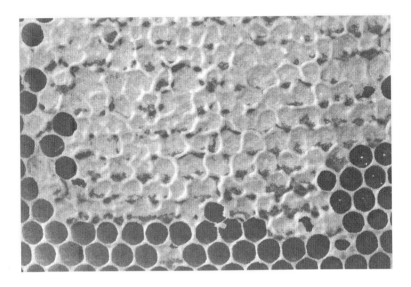

In the above picture, you can see capped honey in the top two-thirds of the image. The bottom third cells are filled with uncapped honey. Uncapped honey can also be extracted provided it is cured. To see whether honey is cured, turn the frame upside down and shake gently. If you can see honey leaking from the cells, then it's not cured yet and shouldn't be extracted. Uncured 'honey' isn't honey as of yet and will spoil your harvest. In this case, put the honey super back into the hive and wait for your bees to cure the remaining honey cells.

When planning on when to harvest your honey, it's important not to wait too long! After the last major nectar flow has ended, your bees will start consuming the honey and much of the honey you were hoping to gravest will be gone. Another thing to keep in mind is temperature. If you wait too long it might be too cold to harvest your honey. Coolness causes honey to thicken which makes it impossible to harvest.

Starting in your second season, you will usually do your first harvest in the middle of summer, usually around late May, and another one in mid-September, before it gets cold. These estimations may however vary from year to year and also depending on where you live. In your second harvest, make sure to lave your bees around 60 to 70 pounds of honey to see them through the winter months. If it's the first season for your colony, you may only have one harvest as the last major nectar flow is coming to an end.

## 2. <u>Removing Honey Supers From the Hive</u>

There are many different ways in which you can extract honey. In this section I will introduce you to the best – and safest – ways of extracting honey. Before harvesting however, make sure to put on your bee-proof clothing and your veil. This is when your bees will most protective so wearing protective globes will also come a long way. Other things you'll need are: your smoker, an empty honey super and an old towel.

1. Open your hive as you would during a routine inspection and use your smoker generously to calm your bees.

2.  Remove the bees from the honey supers. To do this, take a frame at a time and shake the bees off. You can also use a bee brush to brush your bees of the frames. Make sure to only brush upwards so as to avoid hurting any bees. An alternative way in which you can remove your bees from the honey suppers is by using a fume board and bee repellent.
3.  Once you've removed the bees, place the cleared frames into the empty super.
4.  Cover the super with an old towel to prevent your bees from stealing the honey.
5.  Remove the honey suppers from the hive and take them into a bee-free room.

## 3.  <u>Extracting Honey</u>

You should extract your honey as soon as you take the supers off the hive. Once inside, it's therefore time to start extracting your precious honey.

**What You Need:**

- ☐  Uncapping knife, fork or scratcher
- ☐  Honey jars
- ☐  Honey strainer
- ☐  Bottling bucket
- ☐  Honey extractor – An honey extractor is cylindrical piece of equipment (see picture below). An extractor comes in many different sizes and

styles and a good one can be purchased for anywhere between $200 and $500 and upwards. You can purchase budget plastic extractors for cheaper, although I wouldn't recommend using those.

Below are step-by-step instructions on how to extract the honey from your frames:

1.  Uncap the wax-sealed comb cells on both sides of the frame using an uncapping knife, fork or scratcher. I prefer using the uncapping knife first to expose most

cells of honey and then uncap any missed cells with the uncapping fork.

2. Place the uncapped frame vertically into your honey extractor. Once you've uncapped enough frames to fill your extractor, start spinning the frames. The honey will drip to the bottom. Don't spin the frames too fast as this can damage the wax comb.

3. Once both sides of the frames have been emptied, place them back into the honey super.

4. Repeat with the next frames.

5. Open the valve which is located at the bottom of your extractor. This will allow the honey to filter through the stranger into your bottling bucket (see picture below).

6. Bottle your honey in tightly sealed containers!

You are done! It's finally time to enjoy the fruits of your labor. Before storing the honey supers for the winter however, they will have to be cleaned. To clean your extracted frames, place the honey supers on top of your hive (between the top deep hive body and the inner and outer covers) and leave them there for a couple of days. Your bees will lick of all honey residue leaving your frames dry, clean and ready to be stored for the next honey season.

Lastly, before putting your honey supers away for the winter, make sure to treat them with wax moth control either by freezing the combs for at least 24 hours or by treating the supers with PDB crystals.

## 4. **Harvesting Beeswax**

As you extract the honey, the cappings which you slice off are your major wax harvest for the season. The wax can be cleaned and melted to be used in all kinds of DIY projects. You can for example make body lotion or candles; recipes for how to make nourishing body lotion and beeswax candles are to be found in *Section 9.*

**What You Need:**

- ☐ A honey strainer or colander
- ☐ Double boiler
- ☐ Cheesecloth
- ☐ Block mold

**Steps to Follow:**

1. Leave your cappings to drain for a couple of days, allowing as much as honey as possible to drain off them.
2. Wash off any remaining honey from the cuppings using warm water.
3. Drain the cappings through a honey strainer or a colander.
4. Melt the wax by placing the washed cappings in a double boiler.
5. Strain the melted beeswax through cheesecloth to remove any impurities.
6. Pour your wax into the mold and leave your melted wax to set and solidify before removing it. For this, you can use a mold or an old cardboard box, such as a milk carton.

Now that harvesting season is over, it's time to make the most of your harvest! In the next section we will cover some of the fun things you can make and create with your harvest!

# Section 9: DIY Projects and Recipes

In this section, we will cover some of the fun things you can create with your season's harvest. We will cover how you can make nourishing body lotion and how to make homemade beeswax candles!

## 1. **Beeswax Body Lotion**

You can also use your beeswax to make body lotion. Body lotion essentially consists of three elementary elements: oil, water and a binder (called an emulsifier). The emulsifier is what makes the mixture soft and creamy. Below is a very simple recipe which you can experiment with. Make sure that none of the equipment you're using contains aluminum. If you want thicker lotion, add more oil to your mixture. Adding more water to your mixture will result in a lighter lotion.

**What You Need:**

- Storage jars or containers
- Double boiler
- Immersion blender
- Spatula
- Small pot
- Medium and large bowl

## Ingredients:

- ☐ 1 ½ cups of distilled water (can't be tap water)
- ☐ Ice cubes
- ☐ ½ cup (125 ml) of olive oil
- ☐ 2 tablespoons of cosmetic grade beeswax
- ☐ Optional: essential oils for scents

## Steps to Follow:

1. Put both oil and beeswax in a double boiler. Warm over medium-low heat until the beeswax is completely melted.
2. While the oil is warming up, put the water in a small pot and heat until simmering without bringing it to boil.
3. Put the ice cubes into a large bowl.
4. Pour the warm oil-wax mixture into the medium mixing bowl and place the bowl above the ice. Blend the mixture with your immersion blender.
5. Slowly add the water to the mixture and keep blending until the mixture is thick.
6. Scrape the lotion into a jar and store in the fridge.

Natural body lotion will only keep for approximately a month - I always advise making it in small batches. You can play with essential oils as much as you like depending on your scent preferences. Certain oils will also add certain benefits to your moisturizer besides a beautiful scent. Primrose oil for example boosts the moisturizing effect of your lotion and is also known to relieve many symptoms of eczema such as itching and redness.

To further customize your body lotion, you can also try herbal infusions! To customize your lotion with herbs, simply boil the distilled water over herbs, leave to sit for an hour before straining out the herbs!

Below is a list of my favorite essential oils to use in body lotions, as well as some of their added benefits:

- **Rose essential oil:** amazing for dry or aging skin. It also helps refine skin tone and texture.

- **Tea tree essential oil:** does wonders for acne-prone skin and helps regulate oil production.

- **Carrot seed essential oil:** rejuvenates your skin and promotes cell regeneration.

- **Frankincense essential oil:** has anti-inflammatory benefits and does wonders if you're prone to acne. It also helps reduce wrinkles and the appearance of scars.

- **Lavender essential oil:** smells amazing and has relaxing qualities that counter stress. It also helps against scarring, sun spots, and signs of aging.

- **Ylang ylang essential oil:** has a beautiful floral scent. It also controls oil production and helps regenerate skin cells.

- **Neroli essential oil:** amazing for oily and sensitive skin. It helps balance oil production and reduces the appearance or pores.

## 2. <u>DIY Beeswax Candles</u>

Beeswax candles are sweet-smelling and make a delightful home feature and a thoughtful gift. You can even use beeswax candles to make some extra profit on the side, from selling them on local crafts and arts or farmer's market to selling them online on Etsy or on a different platform.

### Molded Candles and Jar Candles

To make molded candles, all you need is your beeswax, cottons wicks, a double boiler and molds. Melt the beeswax, place your wick into the mold and pour the wax into the mold. Leave to cool, remove the mold, and you're all done!

Instead of using a mold, you can also use a mason jar and leave your candle to sit inside the jar! You can also add color or scents if you want!

### Hand-Dipped Beeswax Candles

Hand-dipped candles are absolutely beautiful. All you need is yours beeswax, cotton wicks, a double boiler and a tall container to melt your wax in. To make hand-dipped candles, follow the steps below:

1. Melt the beeswax in a tall container. Keep the container in a hot water bath to keep the wax melted.
2. Take on end of the wicking and start dipping.
3. Leave each layer of wax to cool before dipping it again.
4. Repeat until you have built up the desired thickness.

If you are feeling extra creative, add scents and colors to your wax. Leave your candles to hang for a couple of hours until completely dry.

# Section 10: Last but Not Least

I'd like to take this opportunity to thank you for downloading this book. I hope you now have a solid foundation on the process, and that you're equipped with the knowledge to put you on the path to becoming a proud and self-sufficient beekeeper!

Don't underestimate the importance of backyard beekeeping – not only on you personally, but also on the bee community at large. Backyard beekeeping can help reestablish lost colonies that are currently decreasing. Let's work together to re-build the honey bee population!

My final piece of advice - no matter how diligent you are in your research, your best learning will come from getting started and getting to know your bees. During the first week after hiving, try and observe your bees from a distance and just let them bee! All inspection techniques will become second nature with practice and once you have nailed them down, you can become more and more watchful of the life cycles of your little bees. Honey bees are wonderful creatures and beekeeping is both a job as well as a privilege.

I sincerely wish you the best of luck in your bee-venture!

Best wishes,

Andy Jacobson

14119146R00050

Made in the USA
Lexington, KY
05 November 2018